MW00878256

The Everyday Co
Cookbook with 130 *.
Recipes That are Easy on the Budget

Dedication
To my Mom and Dad - Thank You!

Introduction

In my family we are no strangers to stretching the dollar, living in an ex-Communist country that is still one of the poorest within the EU. We are always living paycheck to paycheck, so we find the cheapest ways possible to cook meals that will feed our family of five. Our menus are strongly influenced by traditional cuisine and contain a lot of simple, hearty foods. When I think about it, every meal in my house is a comfort food and is also cooked with the budget in mind.

Some of our favorite recipes are those inexpensive dishes that we had at home when we were growing up, like Roast Chicken, Chicken and Potatoes, Chicken with Rice, Green Salad, Shredded Egg Salad, Summer Macaroni Salad, Meatloaf, Stuffed Peppers or Meatballs in Tomato Sauce. So today, these meals are frequently on our table and are especially loved by our kids.

There are several ways we stretch the dollar. We make a lot more soups, casseroles and one pot dinners, bean and rice dishes, or stewed vegetables with rice. We also have one or two vegetarian dinners each week because Bulgarian vegetarian food is incredibly healthy, cheap and easy to cook.

We try to buy produce that is seasonally available and, when possible, buy in bulk. We eat lots of greens, potatoes, squash, cabbage and other less pricey vegetables, prepared in a variety of ways. Lentils, beans, green peas and chick peas, are all inexpensive and the recipes to prepare them are also endless. Herbs and spices are a great way to enhance the flavor of a dish without having to spend much at all. The spices we use are not expensive but would be even cheaper if you grow them in pots at your kitchen window.

Another thing to do is buy meat only when on sale and stock up the freezer. We frequently cook egg dishes, meatloaf, meatballs, or different Mediterranean meat and fish recipes that are not only delicious but also budget friendly and healthy.

And because it is not good to throw away food, don't forget to use your leftover fruits and vegetables for health and beauty routines. If an avocado or banana has gone too ripe, use it as a hair or face mask. After saving all this money on food, you deserve a little pampering!

Cooking on a budget doesn't mean you have to sacrifice flavor or nutrition. Cooking on a budget is a skill you learn over time. Yes, it takes a little more time and planning but in the end it turns out that the more you focus on purchasing local, unprocessed food and preparing meals at home, the healthier and tastier your meals will be, and the more money you'll save.

Table Of Contents

9

Salads and Appetizers

Sausage and Pasta Salad

Serves 6

Ingredients:

1 1/2 cup spiral pasta

2 tbsp sunflower oil

1 lb pork sausages

2 zucchinis, sliced lengthwise

1 1/2 cups cherry tomatoes

1 cup small mozzarella cheese, sliced

4 tbsp sunflower oil

4 tbsp lemon juice

1 tsp dried basil

Directions:

Cook pasta, following package directions, or until al dente. Drain and transfer to a bowl. Stir in two tablespoons of oil. Set aside to cool.

Grill sausages, turning, for ten minutes, or until just cooked through. Set aside to cool slightly and slice thickly. Grill zucchinis until char grilled. Transfer to a plate. Grill tomatoes for one minute.

Combine sausages, zucchinis, tomatoes, and mozzarella with pasta. Prepare the dressing by whisking together lemon juice, sunflower oil and basil. Drizzle over salad. Season with salt and pepper and toss to combine. Serve warm.

Potato and Pancetta Salad

Serves 6

Ingredients:

2 lbs spring potatoes, washed, peeled, halved lengthwise

6 slices mild pancetta

1 bunch asparagus, woody ends trimmed, diagonally cut into 2 inch lengths

1/2 cup green beans, cut in 2 inch lengths

2 garlic cloves, crushed

4 tbsp sunflower oil

1 tbsp red wine vinegar

1 tbsp mustard

1/4 cup spring onions, finely cut

salt and black pepper, to taste

Directions:

Preheat oven to 350 F. Combine potatoes, two tablespoons of sunflower oil, and garlic in a large baking dish. Season with salt and pepper to taste and bake, turning occasionally, for about twenty minutes, or until golden brown.

Heat a large frying pan over medium heat. Cook the pancetta slices for one minute each side, or until crisp. Drain and transfer to a plate. Cook the asparagus and green beans in salted boiling water for three minutes, or until bright green and tender crisp. Drain.

Break the pancetta into large pieces. Place in a large serving bowl together with the potatoes, asparagus, green beans and spring onions.

Combine the remaining oil, vinegar and mustard in a small bowl. Season with salt and pepper and drizzle over the salad. Gently toss and serve.

Salmon Macaroni Salad Recipe

Serves 6

Ingredients:

2 cups macaroni pasta

1 cup canned salmon, cut into medium chunks

1 red pepper, cut into strips

1/2 cup canned sweet corn, drained

1/2 cup mayonnaise

1 tsp mustard

1 tsp lemon juice

1 bunch spring onions, chopped

3 tbsp fresh parsley leaves, finely cut

1 tbsp fresh dill, finely cut

freshly ground black pepper, to taste

Directions:

Cook macaroni according to package directions. Remove from heat, drain, rinse briefly in cold water and drain again.

In a large bowl, mix the salmon, corn, red pepper, mayonnaise, mustard, and lemon juice. Mix in the spring onions, parsley and dill. Add the cooked macaroni while still warm. Season with freshly ground pepper to taste. Serve chilled.

White Bean and Tuna Salad

Serves 4

Ingredients:

2 cups canned white beans, rinsed and drained

1 cup canned tuna, cut into large chunks

1 red onion, chopped

1/2 cup black olives, pitted, halved

juice of one lemon

1/2 cup fresh parsley leaves, chopped

1 tbsp dried mint

salt and freshly ground black pepper , to taste

3 tbsp sunflower oil

Directions:

Put tuna into a large bowl. Add the white beans and gently stir to combine. Add olives, onions, parsley, mint, lemon juice and sunflower oil and mix to combine. If the salad seems a little dry, add some more oil.

Season with salt and black pepper to taste. Serve chilled.

Chicken Pasta Salad

Serves 6

Ingredients:

4 cups spiral pasta, cooked

1 small chicken, boiled or roasted, skin and bones removed, shredded or cut into small pieces.

1 cup cherry tomatoes

1 cucumber, halved, sliced

1 yellow bell pepper, sliced

1 red onion, chopped

1/2 cup fresh basil leaves, finely chopped

1/2 cup black olives, pitted

for the dressing

2 tbsp red wine vinegar

4 tbsp sunflower oil

2 garlic cloves, crushed

Directions:

Combine pasta, chicken, tomatoes, cucumber, bell pepper, onion, basil and olives in a large salad bowl.

Make the dressing by mixing vinegar, oil, garlic and salt. Pour the dressing over the salad and toss to combine.

Greek Chicken Salad

Serves 4

Ingredients:

4 small chicken breast halves

juice of one lemon

1-2 tsp fresh rosemary, chopped

3 garlic cloves, crushed

4 tbsp olive oil

2 tomatoes, cut into thin wedges

1 small red onion, cut into thin wedges

1/4 cup black olives, pitted

3.5 oz feta, crumbled

1/4 cup parsley leaves, chopped

Directions:

Prepare the dressing from the lemon juice, garlic, rosemary and olive oil. Place the chicken fillets in a bowl with half the dressing. Stir well and marinate for at least 15 minutes.

Heat a char-grill pan or non-stick frying pan over medium high heat. Cook the chicken for five minutes each side, or until golden and cooked through. Set aside, covered with foil.

Toss the tomatoes, onion, olives, feta and parsley in the remaining dressing. Slice the chicken thickly and add to the salad, then toss gently to combine.

Italian Chicken Salad

Serves 4

Ingredients:

2 chicken breasts, cooked, shredded

2 yellow or orange bell peppers, thinly sliced

1 small red onion, thinly sliced

1 celery rib, chopped

1/4 cup slivered almonds, toasted

1 tbsp drained capers

juice of one lemon

1 tsp fresh thyme, minced

1/3 cup of Parmesan cheese

1/4 cup olive oil

1 tbsp mustard

1 tsp sugar

salt and pepper to taste

Directions:

Combine the vegetables and the chicken in a salad bowl.

Prepare the dressing by mixing the olive oil, lemon juice, mustard, sugar, salt and pepper and pour over the salad. Stir well to combine and serve.

Chicken and Green Pea Salad

Serves 4

Ingredients:

2 cups chicken breast, cooked and chopped

1 cup green peas, cooked, drained

1 medium apple, diced

1 garlic clove, crushed

2-3 spring onions, finely cut

1/3 cup fresh dill, finely cut

salt and ground black pepper to taste

2 tbsp lemon juice

2 tbsp sunflower oil

Directions:

Combine all salad ingredients in a bowl and mix well. Serve chilled.

Chicken and Egg Salad

Serves 6

Ingredients:

2 cups cooked chicken, chopped

2 hard boiled eggs, diced

2-3 pickled gherkins, chopped

1 large apple, diced

1/2 cup walnuts, baked

1/2 cup light mayonnaise

1 tbsp lemon juice

salt and pepper to taste

Directions:

Bake walnuts in a single layer in a preheated to 450 F oven for 3 minutes, or until toasted and fragrant, stirring halfway through.

Stir together chicken, apple, eggs and gherkins. Combine mayonnaise, lemon juice, salt and pepper to taste, and add to the chicken mixture. Sprinkle with walnuts and serve.

Summer Macaroni Salad

Serves 6

Ingredients:

2 cups macaroni pasta

2 hard boiled eggs, chopped

2 roasted red bell peppers, thinly sliced

3 tbsp fresh dill, chopped

3-4 spring onions, finely cut

1/3 cup mayonnaise

2 tbsp lemon juice

freshly ground black pepper, to taste

Directions:

Cook macaroni, as directed on package. When cooked through but still slightly firm remove from heat, drain and rinse with cool water.

Put chopped onions into a salad bowl and toss with the lemon juice. Add in macaroni and all other ingredients. Season with salt and pepper to taste and serve.

Greek Salad

Serves 6

Ingredients:

2 cucumbers, diced

2 tomatoes, sliced

1 green lettuce, cut in thin strips

2 red bell peppers, cut

1/2 cup black olives, pitted

3.5 oz feta cheese, cut

1 red onion, sliced

2 tbsp olive oil

2 tbsp lemon juice

salt and ground black pepper

Directions:

Dice the cucumbers and slice the tomatoes. Tear the lettuce or cut it in thin strips. De-seed and cut the peppers in strips.

Mix all vegetables in a salad bowl. Add the olives and the feta cheese cut in cubes.

In a small cup mix the olive oil and the lemon juice with salt and pepper. Pour over the salad and stir again.

Apple, Celery and Walnut Salad

Serves 4

Ingredients:

4 apples, quartered, cores removed, thinly sliced

1 celery rib, thinly sliced

1/2 cup walnuts, chopped

2 tbsp raisins

1 large red onion, thinly sliced

3 tbsp apple cider vinegar

2 tbsp sunflower oil

Directions:

Combine vinegar, oil, salt and pepper in a small bowl. Whisk until well combined.

Combine apples, celery, walnuts, raisins and onion in a large salad bowl. Drizzle with the dressing and toss gently to combine.

Caprese Salad

Serves 6

Ingredients:

4 tomatoes, sliced

6 oz mozzarella cheese, sliced

10 fresh basil leaves

3 tbsp olive oil

2 tbsp red wine vinegar

salt to taste

Directions:

Slice the tomatoes and mozzarella, then layer the tomato slices, whole fresh basil leaves and mozzarella slices on a plate.

Drizzle olive oil and vinegar over the salad and serve.

Beet and Bean Sprout Salad

Serves 4

Ingredients:

7 beet greens, finely sliced

2 medium tomatoes, cut into wedges

1 cup bean sprouts, washed

1 tbsp grated lemon rind

2 garlic cloves, crushed

1/2 cup lemon juice

1/3 cup olive oil

1 tsp salt

Directions:

In a large bowl toss together beet greens, bean sprouts and tomatoes.

Prepare a dressing from the oil, lemon juice, lemon rind, salt and garlic and pour it over the salad. Refrigerate for 2 hours to allow the flavor to develop before serving. Serve chilled.

Asian Coleslaw

Serves 4

Ingredients:

for the salad

1/2 Chinese cabbage, shredded

1 green bell pepper, sliced into thin strips

1 carrot, cut into thin strips

4 spring onions, chopped

for the dressing

3 tbsp lemon juice

3 tbsp soy sauce

3 tbsp sweet chilly sauce

Directions:

Remove any damaged outer leaves and rinse cabbage. Holding cabbage from the base and, starting at the opposite end, shred leaves thinly.

Combine vegetables first, then the dressing ingredients. Pour over the salad and toss well.

Shredded Egg Salad

Serves 4

Ingredients:

3 large hard boiled eggs, shredded

2-3 spring onions, finely cut

2-3 garlic cloves, crushed

4 tbsp mayonnaise

1 tbsp mustard

1 tbsp yogurt

1 salt and pepper, to taste

Directions:

Peel the shell off of the eggs. Shred the eggs in a medium salad bowl. Mix the remaining ingredients. Serve chilled.

Baby Spinach Salad

Serves 4

Ingredients:

1 bag baby spinach, washed and dried

9 oz feta cheese, coarsely crumbled

1 red bell pepper, cut in slices

1 cup cherry tomatoes, halved

1 red onion, finely chopped

1 cup black olives, pitted

1 tsp dried oregano

1 large garlic clove

3 tbsp red wine vinegar

4 tbsp olive oil

salt and freshly ground black pepper to taste

Directions:

Prepare the dressing by blending the garlic and the oregano with the olive oil and the vinegar in a food processor.

Place the spinach leaves in a large salad bowl and toss with the dressing. Add the rest of the ingredients and give everything a toss again. Season to taste with black pepper and salt.

Tabbouleh

Serves 6

Ingredients:

1 cup raw bulgur

2 cups boiling water

a bunch of parsley, finely cut

2 tomatoes, chopped

3 tbsp olive oil

2 garlic cloves, minced

6-7 fresh onions, chopped

10 fresh mint leaves, chopped

juice of two lemons

salt and black pepper

Directions:

Bring water and salt to a boil, then pour over bulgur. Cover and set aside for 15 minutes to steam. Drain excess water from bulgur and fluff with a fork. Leave to cool.

In a large bowl, mix together the parsley, tomatoes, olive oil, garlic, spring onions and mint. Stir in the cooled bulgur and season to taste with salt, pepper, and lemon juice.

Fatoush

Serves 6

Ingredients:

2 cups lettuce, washed, dried, and chopped

3 tomatoes, chopped

1 cucumber, peeled and chopped

1 green pepper, deseeded and chopped

1 cup radishes, sliced in half

1 small red onion, finely chopped

half a bunch of parsley, finely cut

2 tbsp finely chopped fresh mint

3 tbsp olive oil

4 tbsp lemon juice

salt and black pepper to taste

2 whole-wheat pita breads

Directions:

Toast the pita breads in a skillet until they are browned and crisp. Set aside.

Place the lettuce, tomatoes, cucumbers, green pepper, radishes, onion, parsley and mint in a salad bowl. Break up the toasted pita into bite-size pieces and add to the salad.

Make the dressing by whisking together the olive oil with the lemon juice, a pinch of salt and some black pepper. Toss everything together until well is coated with dressing and serve.

The Best Orzo Salad

Serves 6

Ingredients:

for the dressing:

1/3 cup olive oil

3/4 cup fresh lemon juice

1 tbsp dried mint

for the salad:

1 cup uncooked orzo

2 tbsp olive oil

a bunch of fresh onions, chopped

3 green peppers, diced

1/2 cup black olives, pitted, cut

2 tomatoes, diced

1 cup raw sunflower seeds

Directions:

The dressing: Combine olive oil, lemon juice, and mint in a small bowl, mixing well. Place the dressing in the refrigerator until ready to use.

Cook the orzo according to package directions (in salted water) and rinse thoroughly with cold water when you strain it. Transfer to a large bowl and toss with the olive oil. Allow orzo to cool completely.

Once orzo is cooled, add the diced peppers, finely cut fresh onions, olives and diced tomatoes stirring until mixed well. Stir the dressing (it will have separated by this point) and add it to the salad, tossing to evenly coat. Add salt and pepper to taste and sprinkle with sunflower seeds.

Chickpea Salad

Serves 4

Ingredients:

1 cup canned chickpeas, drained and rinsed

2 spring onions, thinly sliced

1 small cucumber, diced

2 green bell peppers, chopped

2 tomatoes, diced

2 tbsp chopped fresh parsley

1 tsp capers, drained and rinsed

juice of half lemon

2 tbsp sunflower oil

1 tbsp red wine vinegar

salt and pepper to taste

a pinch of dried oregano

Directions:

In a medium bowl, toss together the chickpeas, spring onions, cucumber, bell pepper, tomato, parsley, capers, and lemon juice.

In a smaller bowl stir together the remaining ingredients and pour over the chickpea salad. Toss well to coat and allow to marinate, stirring occasionally, for at least one hour before serving.

Green Lettuce Salad

Serves 4

Ingredients:

1 green lettuce, washed and drained

1 cucumber, sliced

a bunch of radishes

a bunch of spring onions

the juice of half a lemon or 2 tbsp of white wine vinegar

3 tbsp sunflower or olive oil

salt to taste

Directions:

Cut the lettuce into thin strips. Slice the cucumber and the radishes as thinly as possible and chop the spring onions.

Mix all the salad ingredients in a large bowl, add the lemon juice and oil and season with salt to taste.

Fried Zucchinis with Tomato Sauce

Serves 4

Ingredients:

4 zucchinis medium size

1 cup all purpose flour

2 cups sunflower oil for frying

salt

for the tomato sauce

4-5 ripe tomatoes, skinned and grated

1 carrot

1/2 onion

2 cloves garlic, whole

1 tsp salt

1/2 sunflower oil

1 tsp sugar

3 tbsp flour

1/2 bunch fresh parsley

Directions:

Wash and peel the zucchinis, and cut them in thin diagonal slices or in rings 1/4 inch thick. Salt and leave them in a suitable bowl placing it inclined to drain away the juices.

Coat the zucchinis with flour, then fry turning on both sides until they are golden-brown (about 3 minutes on each side). Transfer to paper towels and pat dry.

Heat the oil in a large skillet and cook the onion and the carrot until soft. Add the grated tomatoes together with two whole garlic cloves. Season with salt and a tsp of sugar.

Simmer in low heat until thick and ready. Sprinkle with parsley and pour over the fried zucchinis.

Zucchini Bake

Serves 4

Ingredients:

5 medium zucchinis, grated

1 carrot, grated

1 small tomato, diced

1 onion, halved, thinly sliced

2 garlic cloves, crushed

1 cup self-raising flour, sifted

5 eggs, lightly whisked

1/2 cup sunflower oil

1/2 cup fresh dill, finely cut

1 cup grated feta cheese

2 cups yogurt, to serve (optional)

Directions:

Preheat oven to 350 F. Grease and a round, 8 inch base, baking dish.

Combine zucchinis, carrot, tomato, onion, garlic and dill in a bowl. Add flour, eggs, oil and cheese. Season and stir until well combined.

Bake for 30-40 minutes. Serve with yogurt.

Potato Salad

Serves 5-6

Ingredients:

4-5 large potatoes

2-3 spring onions, finely chopped

juice of half a lemon

1/4 cup sunflower or olive oil

salt and pepper to taste

fresh parsley, to serve

Directions:

Peel and boil the potatoes for about 20-25 minutes, drain and leave to cool.

In a salad bowl add the finely chopped spring onions, the lemon juice, salt, pepper and olive oil, and mix gently. Cut the potatoes into cubes and add to the salad bowl.

Gently mix all ingredients and sprinkle with parsley. Serve cold.

Cabbage Salad

Serves 4

Ingredients:

9 oz fresh white cabbage, shredded

9 oz carrots, shredded

9 oz white turnips, shredded

1/2 a bunch of parsley

2 tbsp white vinegar

3 tbsp sunflower oil

salt

Directions:

Combine first three ingredients in a large bowl and mix well. Add salt, vinegar and oil. Stir and sprinkle with parsley.

Red Cabbage Salad

Serves 6

Ingredients:

1 small head red cabbage, cored and chopped

a bunch of fresh dill, finely cut

3 tbsp sunflower oil

3 tbsp red wine vinegar

1 tsp white sugar

2 tbsp salt

black pepper, to taste

Directions:

In a small bowl, mix the oil, red wine vinegar, sugar and black pepper. Place the cabbage in a large salad bowl. Sprinkle the salt on top and crunch it with your hands to soften.

Pour the dressing over the cabbage, and toss to coat. Sprinkle the salad with dill, cover it with foil and leave it in the refrigerator for half an hour before serving.

Okra Salad

Serves 4

Ingredients:

1 lb young okras

juice from 1 lemon

1/2 bunch of parsley, chopped

2 hard tomatoes

3 tbsp sunflower oil

1/2 tsp black pepper

salt

Directions:

Trim okras, wash and cook in salted water. Drain and cool when tender.

In a small bowl mix well the lemon juice and sunflower oil, salt and pepper. Pour over the okras arranged in a bowl and sprinkle with chopped parsley.

Wash tomatoes and cut them into slices, then garnish the salad with them.

Cucumber Salad

Serves 4

Ingredients:

2 medium cucumbers, sliced

a bunch of fresh dill

2 cloves garlic

3 tbsp white vinegar

5 tbsp olive oil

salt to taste

Directions:

Cut the cucumbers in rings and put arrange them on a plate. Add the finely cut dill, the pressed garlic and season with salt, vinegar and oil. Mix well and serve cold.

Beetroot Salad

Serves 4

Ingredients:

2-3 small beets, peeled

3 spring onions, chopped

3 garlic cloves, pressed

2 tbsp red wine vinegar

2-3 tbsp sunflower oil

salt to taste

Directions:

Place the beats in a steam basket set over a pot of boiling water. Steam for about 15-20 minutes, or until tender. Leave to cool.

Grate the beets and put them in a salad bowl. Add the crushed garlic cloves, the finely cut spring onions and mix well. Season with salt, vinegar and sunflower oil.

Tomato Couscous Salad

Serves 2

Ingredients:

1 cup medium couscous

1 cup hot water

2 ripe tomatoes, diced

1/2 red onion, finely cut

5 tbsp sunflower oil

4 tbsp lemon juice

1 tbsp dry mint

Directions:

Place the couscous in a large bowl. Boil water with one tablespoon of olive oil and pour over the couscous. Cover and set aside for 10 minutes. Fluff couscous with a fork and when it is completely cold, stir in the tomatoes, onion and dry mint.

In a separate small bowl, combine the remaining olive oil, the lemon juice and salt, add to the couscous and stir until well combined.

Carrot Salad

Serves 4

Ingredients:

4 carrots, shredded

1 apple, peeled, cored and shredded

2 garlic cloves, crushed

2 tbsp lemon juice

2 tbsp honey

salt and pepper to taste

Directions:

In a bowl, combine the shredded carrots, apple, lemon juice, honey, garlic, salt and pepper. Toss and chill before serving.

Bulgur Salad

Serves 4

Ingredients:

1 cup bulgur

2 cups boiling water

3 tbsp olive oil

1/2 cup black olives, pitted, halved

1 tomato, chopped

2-3 spring onions, finely cut

2 tbsp lemon zest

juice from two lemons

2 tbsp fresh mint, finely chopped

4 tbsp fresh parsley, finely chopped

salt and black pepper to taste

Directions:

In a large bowl, pour boiling water over bulgur. Stir in olive oil, lemon zest, lemon juice, mint and parsley and leave aside for 30 minutes.

Fluff bulgur with a fork and add the chopped tomato, onions and olives. Season with salt and pepper to taste.

Roasted Eggplant and Pepper Salad

Serves 4

Ingredients:

2 medium eggplants

2 red or green bell peppers

2 tomatoes

3 cloves garlic, crushed

fresh parsley

1-2 tbsp red wine vinegar

olive oil, as needed

salt, pepper

Directions:

Wash and dry the vegetables. Prick the skin off the eggplants. Bake the eggplants, tomatoes and peppers in a pre-heated oven at 480 F for about 40 minutes, until the skins are well burnt.

Take out of the oven and leave in a covered container for about 10 minutes. Peel the skins off and drain well the extra juices. De-seed the peppers. Cut all the vegetables into tiny pieces. Add the garlic and stir to combine. Add the olive oil, vinegar and salt to taste. Stir again. Serve cold and sprinkled with parsley.

Green Bean Salad

Serves 6

Ingredients:

2 cups green beans, cooked

1 onion, sliced

4 garlic cloves, crushed

1 tbsp fresh mint, chopped

1 bunch of fresh dill, finely chopped

3 tbsp olive oil

1 tablespoon apple cider vinegar

salt and pepper to taste

Directions:

Pour the green beans in a medium bowl and mix them with onion, mint and dill.

In a smaller bowl combine olive oil, vinegar, garlic, salt, and pepper. Toss into the green bean mixture.

Zucchini Pasta Salad

Serves 6

Ingredients:

2 cups spiral pasta

2 zucchinis, sliced and halved

4 tomatoes, cut

1 cup white mushrooms, cut

1 small red onion, chopped

2 tbsp fresh basil leaves, chopped

3.5 oz blue cheese

2 tbsp sunflower oil

1 tbsp lemon juice

black pepper, to taste

Directions:

Cook pasta according to directions, or until al dente. Drain, rinse with cold water and drain again.

Place zucchinis, tomatoes, mushrooms and onion in a large bowl. Add pasta and mix gently. Combine oil, lemon juice, basil, blue cheese and black pepper in a blender. Pour over salad. Toss gently and serve.

Russian Salad

Serves 6

Ingredients:

3 potatoes, boiled, cut

2 carrots, boiled, cut

1 cup canned green peas, drained

6 oz ham, cut

1 cup mayonnaise

5 pickled gherkins, chopped

black olives, to serve

salt to taste

Directions:

Boil the potatoes and carrots, then chop into small cubes. Put everything, except for the mayonnaise, in a serving bowl and mix.

Add salt to taste, then stir in the mayonnaise. Garnish with parsley and olives. Serve cold.

White Bean Salad

Serves 4-5

Ingredients:

1 cup dry white beans

1 onion, whole

5-6 spring onions, chopped

3 tbsp white wine vinegar

a bunch of fresh parsley, finely cut

salt and black pepper, to taste

Directions:

Wash the beans and soak them in cold water to swell overnight. Cook in the same water with the peeled onion. When tender, drain and put into a deeper bowl. Remove the onion.

Mix well oil, vinegar, salt and pepper. Pour over the still warm beans, leave to cool about 30-40 minutes.

Chop the spring onions and the parsley, add to the beans, mix and leave to cool for at least 40 minutes. Serve cold.

Soups

Bulgarian Beef Soup

Serves 6

Ingredients:

1.5 lbs beef shin, cut into large pieces

6 cups of water

3 carrots, peeled and cut into 3-inch pieces

2 large onions, peeled and quartered

5 potatoes, peeled and quartered

1 celery rib, chopped

1 bay leaf

2 tsp salt

1 tsp black pepper

3 tbsp oil

a bunch of fresh parsley, chopped

Directions:

Add six cups of water to a large heavy-bottomed soup pot. Add the beef, bay leaf, onions, carrots, salt and pepper and bring to a boil. Reduce heat and cover partially with a lid. Simmer for 2-3 hours, adding water if necessary.

Add the potatoes and celery, and bring back to a boil. Simmer for 30 minutes. Serve hot, garnished with fresh parsley.

Italian Meatball Soup

Serves 8

Ingredients:

1 lb lean ground beef

1 small onion, grated

1 onion, chopped

2 garlic cloves, crushed

1/2 cup fresh white breadcrumbs

3-4 basil leaves, finely chopped

1/3 cup Parmesan cheese, grated

1 egg, lightly beaten

2 cups tomato sauce with basil

3 cups water

1/2 cup small pasta

1 zucchini, diced

1/2 cup green beans, trimmed, cut into thirds

2 tbsp olive oil

Directions:

Combine ground beef, grated onion, garlic, breadcrumbs, basil, Parmesan and egg in a large bowl. Season with salt and pepper.

Mix well with hands and roll tablespoonfuls of the mixture into balls. Place on a large plate.

Heat olive oil into a large deep saucepan and sauté onion and garlic until transparent. Add tomato sauce, water and bring to the boil over high heat. Add meatballs. Reduce heat to medium-low and simmer, uncovered, for 10 minutes. Add pasta and cook for five more minutes. Add the zucchini and beans. Cook until pasta and vegetables are tender.

Bulgarian Meatball Soup

Serves 8-10

Ingredients:

1 lb lean ground beef (or 60% pork+40% beef)

3-4 tbsp flour

1 onion, chopped

2 garlic cloves, cut

1 tomato, diced

2 potatoes, diced

1 carrot, diced

1 green pepper, chopped

4 cups water

5.5 oz vermicelli, broken into pieces

1/2 bunch of parsley, finely cut

3 tbsp sunflower oil

1/2 tsp black pepper

1 tsp savory

1 tsp paprika

1 tsp salt

Directions:

Combine ground meat, savory, paprika, black pepper and salt in a large bowl. Mix well with hands and roll teaspoonfuls of the mixture into balls. Put flour in a small bowl and roll each meatball in the flour, coating entire surface then set aside on a large plate.

Heat oil into a large soup pot and sauté onion and garlic until transparent. Add water and bring to the boil over high heat. Add meatballs, carrot, green pepper and potatoes.

Reduce heat to low and simmer, uncovered, for 15 minutes. Add tomato, parsley and vermicelli and cook for 5 more minutes.

Serve with a dollop of yogurt on top.

Beef and Vegetable Minestrone

Serves 8

Ingredients

2 slices bacon, chopped

1 cup lean ground beef

2 carrots, chopped

2 cloves garlic, finely chopped

1 large onion, chopped

1 celery rib, chopped

1 bay leaf

1 tsp dried basil

1 tsp dried rosemary, crushed

1/4 tsp crushed chillies

1 can tomatoes, chopped

1 cup beef broth

2 cups water

1 cup canned chickpeas, drained

1/2 cup small pasta

Directions:

In a large saucepan, cook bacon and ground beef until well done, breaking up the beef as it cooks. Drain off the fat and add carrots, garlic, onion and celery.

Cook for about five minutes or until the onions are translucent. Season with the bay leaf, basil and rosemary. Stir in tomatoes, water and beef broth.

Bring to a boil then reduce heat and simmer for about 20 minutes. Add the chickpeas and pasta.

Cook uncovered, for about 10 minutes or until the pasta is ready.

Mediterranean Chicken Soup

Serves 6

Ingredients:

about 1 lb chicken breasts

3-4 carrots, chopped

1 celery rib, chopped

1 red onion, chopped

1/3 cup rice

6 cups water

10 black olives, pitted and halved

fresh parsley or coriander, to serve

1/2 tsp salt

ground black pepper, to taste

lemon juice, to serve

Directions:

Place chicken breasts in a soup pot. Add onion, carrots, celery, salt, pepper and water. Stir well and bring to a boil. Add rice, olives, stir and reduce heat. Simmer for 30-40 minutes.

Remove chicken from pot and let it cool slightly. Shred it and return it to pot. Serve soup with lemon juice and sprinkled with fresh parsley or coriander.

Greek Lemon Chicken Soup

Serves 6

Ingredients:

12 oz uncooked boneless, skinless chicken breast, diced

1/3 cup rice

2 cups chicken broth

1 cup water

1 onion, finely diced

2 raw eggs

3 tbsp olive oil

1/2 cup fresh lemon juice

1 tablespoon salt

1 tsp ground pepper

a bunch of fresh parsley for garnish, finely cut

Directions:

In a medium pot, heat the olive oil and sauté the onions until they are soft and translucent. Add the chicken broth and water together with the washed rice and bring everything to a boil then reduce heat. When the rice is almost done, add the diced chicken breast to the pot. Let it cook for another 5 minutes or until the chicken is cooked through.

In a small bowl, beat the eggs and lemon juice together. Pour two cups of broth slowly into the egg mixture, whisking constantly. When all the broth is incorporated, add this mixture into the pot of chicken soup and stir well to blend. Do not boil any more.

Season with salt and pepper and garnish with parsley. Serve hot.

Bean, Chicken and Sausage Soup

Serves 8

Ingredients:

10.5 oz Italian sausage

3 bacon strips, diced

2 cups chicken, cooked and diced

1 cup canned kidney beans, rinsed and drained

1 big onion, chopped

2 garlic cloves, crushed

3 cups water

1 cup canned tomatoes, diced, undrained

1 bay leave

1 tsp dried thyme

1 tsp savory

1/2 tsp dried basil

salt and pepper to taste

Directions:

Cook the sausage, onion and bacon over medium heat until sausage is not longer pink. Drain off the fat. Add the garlic and cook for a minute.

Add the water, tomatoes and seasonings and bring to a boil. Cover, reduce heat and simmer for 30 minutes. Add chicken and beans. Simmer for 5 minutes.

Moroccan Chicken and Butternut Squash Soup

Serves 8

Ingredients:

3 skinless, boneless chicken thighs (about 14 oz), cut into bite-sized pieces

1 big onion, chopped

1 zucchini, quartered lengthwise and sliced into 1/2-inch pieces

3 cups peeled butternut squash, cut in 1/2-inch pieces

2 tbsp tomato paste

4 cups chicken broth

1/3 cup uncooked couscous

1/2 tsp ground cumin

1/4 tsp ground cinnamon

1 tsp paprika

1 tsp salt

2 tbsp fresh basil leaves, chopped

1 tbsp grated orange rind

3 tbsp olive oil

Directions:

Heat a soup pot over medium heat. Gently sauté onion, for 3-4 minutes, stirring occasionally. Add chicken pieces and cook for 3-4 minutes, until chicken is brown on all sides.

Add cumin, cinnamon, and paprika and stir well. Add butternut squash and tomato paste; stir again. Add chicken broth and bring to a boil then reduce heat, and simmer 10 minutes.

Stir in couscous, salt, and zucchini pieces; cook until squash is tender.

Remove pot from heat. Season with salt and pepper to taste. Stir in chopped basil and orange rind and serve.

Chicken Soup with Vermicelli

Serves 4

Ingredients:

1 whole chicken leg or 1/2 lb chicken breast

1/2 cup vermicelli

1 carrot, grated

4 cups water

3 cloves of garlic, sliced

1 tsp salt

1/2 tsp black pepper

1 egg, beaten

2 tbsp lemon juice

Directions:

Place the chicken in a pot and add 4 cups of water. Add 1 tsp salt and boil until the chicken is cooked. Take the chicken out of the pot, let it cool a little and cut it into bite size pieces.

Add carrot and garlic to the soup and bring it to a boil. Add vermicelli and chicken pieces. Reduce heat and simmer over medium heat for 8-10 minutes. When ready let it cool for a while.

Mix the beaten egg and lemon juice in a bowl and slowly stir into the soup. Do not boil it again. Serve soup warm, seasoned with black pepper to taste.

Balkan Chicken Soup

Serves 8 - 10

Ingredients:

1 whole chicken (3-4 lbs), cut into sections

1 large onion, whole

1 large onion, chopped

3 garlic cloves, chopped

2 carrots, chopped

1 red bell pepper

1 tsp thyme

2 bay leaves

2 tbsp olive oil

1 tsp salt

black pepper to taste

1 tbsp savory

Directions:

Place the chicken, bay leaves, salt, whole onion and whole red pepper into a pot with five cups of cold water. Bring the pot to boil, reduce heat and simmer for one hour, scooping out any solid foam that settles at the top. When ready, strain the broth and reserve.

Remove the meat from the chicken and cut into large chunks. Discard the bay leafs, the onion and the pepper. Place the pot back on the stove, heat the olive oil and sauté the other onion, garlic, carrots and thyme for about 5 minutes. Pour in the broth and season with salt and pepper.

Simmer for about 15 minutes or until the vegetables are tender. Add in the chicken pieces and the oregano. Simmer for 10 more minutes and serve warm.

Brown Lentil Soup

Serves:10

Ingredients:

2 cups brown lentils

2 onions, chopped

5-6 cloves garlic, peeled

3 medium carrots, chopped

2-3 medium tomatoes, ripe

3-4 cups of water

4 tbsp olive oil

1 1/2 tsp paprika

1 tsp summer savory

Directions:

Heat the oil in a cooking pot, add the onions and carrots and sauté until golden. Add the paprika and washed lentils with 3-4 cups of warm water; continue to simmer.

Chop tomatoes and add them to the soup about 15 min after the lentils have started to simmer. Add savory and peeled garlic cloves. Let the soup simmer until the lentils are soft. Salt to taste.

Moroccan Lentil Soup

Serves 10

Ingredients:

1 cup red lentils

1 cup canned chickpeas, drained

2 onions, chopped

2 cloves garlic, minced

1 can chopped tomatoes

1 can white beans

3 carrots, diced

3 celery ribs, diced

4 cups water

1 tsp ginger, grated

1 tsp ground cardamom

1/2 tsp ground cumin

3 tbsp olive oil

Directions:

In large pot, sauté onions, garlic and ginger in olive oil for about 5 minutes. Add the water, lentils, chickpeas, white beans, tomatoes, carrots, celery, cardamom and cumin.

Bring to a boil for a few minutes then simmer for 1/2 hour or longer, until the lentils are tender.

Puree half the soup in a food processor or blender. Return the pureed soup to the pot, stir and serve.

Bean and Pasta Soup

Serves 6-7

Ingredients:

1 cup small pasta, cooked

1 can white beans, rinsed and drained

2 medium carrots, cut

1 cup fresh spinach , torn

1 medium onion, chopped

1 celery rib, chopped

2 garlic cloves, crushed

2 cups water

1 can tomatoes, diced and undrained

1 cup vegetable broth

1/2 tsp rosemary

1/2 tsp basil

3 tbsp olive oil

salt and pepper to taste

Directions:

Heat the olive oil over medium heat and sauté the onion, carrots and celery. Add the garlic and cook for a minute longer. Stir in the water, tomatoes, vegetable broth, basil, rosemary, salt and pepper.

Bring to a boil then reduce heat and simmer for 10 minutes or until the carrots are tender. Drain pasta and add it to the vegetables. Add the beans and spinach and cook until spinach is wilted.

White Bean Soup

Serves 6

Ingredients:

1 cup white beans

2-3 carrots

2 onions, finely chopped

1-2 tomatoes, grated

1 red bell pepper, chopped

4-5 springs of fresh mint and parsley

1 tsp paprika

3 tbsp sunflower oil

salt

Directions:

Soak the beans in cold water for 3-4 hours, drain and discard the water. Cover the beans with cold water. Add the oil, finely chopped carrots, onions and pepper.

Bring to the boil and simmer until the beans are tender. Add the grated tomatoes, mint, paprika and salt. Simmer for another 15 minutes. Serve sprinkled with finely chopped parsley.

Creamy Zucchini Soup

Serves 4

Ingredients:

1 onion, finely chopped

2 garlic cloves, crushed

1 cup vegetable broth

1 cup water

5 zucchinis, peeled, thinly sliced

1 big potato, chopped

1/4 cup fresh basil leaves

1 tsp sugar

1/2 cup yogurt, to serve

Parmesan cheese, to serve

Directions:

Heat oil in a saucepan over medium heat and sauté the onion and garlic, stirring, for 2-3 minutes or until soft.

Add vegetable broth and water and bring to the boil then reduce heat to medium low. Add zucchinis, the potato, a tsp of sugar, and simmer, stirring occasionally, for 10 minutes or until the zucchinis are soft.

Add basil and simmer for 2-3 minutes. Set aside to cool then blend in batches and reheat soup. Serve with a dollop of yogurt and/or sprinkled with Parmesan cheese.

Broccoli, Zucchini and Blue Cheese Soup

Serves 6

Ingredients:

2 leeks, white part only, sliced

1 head broccoli, coarsely chopped

2 zucchinis, chopped

1 potato, chopped

2 cups vegetable broth

2 cups water

3 tbsp olive oil

3.5 oz blue cheese, crumbled

1/3 cup light cream

Directions:

Heat the oil in a large saucepan over medium heat. Sauté the leeks, stirring, for 5 minutes or until soft. Add bite sized pieces of broccoli, zucchinis, potato, water and broth and bring to a boil.

Reduce heat to low and simmer, stirring occasionally, for 10 minutes or until vegetables are just tender. Remove from heat and set aside for 5 minutes to cool slightly.

Transfer soup to a blender. Add the cheese and blend in batches until smooth. Return to saucepan and place over low heat. Add cream and stir to combine. Season with salt and pepper to taste.

Beetroot and Carrot Soup

Serves 6

Ingredients:

4 beets, washed and peeled

2 carrots, peeled, chopped

2 potatoes, peeled, chopped

1 medium onion, chopped

2 cups vegetable broth

2 cups water

2 tbsp yogurt

2 tbsp olive oil

a bunch or spring onions, cut, to serve

Directions:

Peel and chop the beets. Heat olive oil in a saucepan over medium high heat and sauté onion and carrot until onion is tender. Add beets, potatoes, broth and water.

Bring to the boil. Reduce heat to medium and simmer, partially covered, for 30 - 40 minutes or until beets are tender. Cool slightly.

Blend soup in batches, until smooth. Return it to pan over low heat and cook, stirring, for 4 to 5 minutes or until heated through.

Season with salt and pepper. Serve soup topped with yogurt and sprinkled with spring onions.

Borscht

Serves 6

Ingredients:

4 beets, peeled, quartered

1 carrot, peeled, chopped

1 parsnip, peeled, cut into chunks

1 leek, white part only, sliced

1 onion, chopped

1/3 cup lemon juice

1/2 tsp nutmeg

3 bay leaves

6 cups vegetable broth

1 cup sour cream

2-3 dill springs, chopped

Directions:

Place the beets, carrot, parsnip, leek, onion, lemon juice, spices and bay leaves in a large saucepan with the vegetable broth. Bring to the boil, then reduce the heat to low and simmer, partially covered, for 1 1/2 hours.

Cool slightly, then blend in batches and season well with salt and pepper. Return to saucepan and gently heat through. Place in bowls and garnish with sour cream and dill.

Curried Parsnip Soup

Serves 6

Ingredients:

1.5 lb parsnips, peeled, chopped

2 onions, chopped

2 garlic cloves, cut

3 tbsp olive oil

1 tbs curry powder

1/2 cup heavy cream

salt and freshly ground pepper

Directions:

Sauté the onion and garlic together with the curry powder in a large saucepan. Stir in the parsnips and cook, stirring often, for 10 minutes. Add 6 cups of water, bring to the boil and simmer for 30 minutes or until the parsnips are tender.

Set aside to cool then blend in batches until smooth. Return soup to pan over low heat and stir in the cream. Do not boil - only heat through. Season with salt and pepper.

Pumpkin and Bell Pepper Soup

Serves 4

Ingredients:

1 medium leek, chopped

9 oz pumpkin, peeled, deseeded, cut into small cubes

1/2 red bell pepper, cut into small pieces

1 can tomatoes, undrained, crushed

2 cups vegetable broth

1/2 tsp ground cumin

salt and black pepper, to taste

Directions:

Heat the olive oil in a medium saucepan and sauté the leek for 4-5 minutes. Add the pumpkin and bell pepper and cook, stirring, for 2-3 minutes. Add tomatoes, broth and cumin and bring to the boil.

Cover, reduce heat to low and simmer, stirring occasionally, for 30 minutes or until vegetables are soft. Season with salt and pepper and leave aside to cool.

Blend in batches and re-heat to serve.

Moroccan Pumpkin Soup

Serves 6

Ingredients :

1 leek, white part only, thinly sliced

3 cloves garlic, finely chopped

1/2 tsp ground ginger

1/2 tsp ground cinnamon

1/2 tsp ground cumin

2 carrots, peeled, coarsely chopped

2 lbs pumpkin, peeled, deseeded, diced

1/3 cup chick peas

5 tbsp olive oil

Juice of 1/2 lemon

parsley springs, to serve

Directions:

Heat oil in a large saucepan and sauté leek and garlic with 2 tsp salt, stirring occasionally, until soft. Add, cinnamon, ginger and cumin and stir again. Add carrots, pumpkin chick peas and 5 cups of water to saucepan and bring to the boil.

Reduce heat and simmer for 50 minutes or until chick peas are soft. Remove from heat, add lemon juice and blend soup, in batches, until smooth.

Return it to pan over low heat and cook, stirring, for 4 to 5 minutes or until heated through. Serve topped with parsley sprigs.

Spinach, Leek and Rice Soup

Serves 6

Ingredients:

2 leeks halved lengthwise and sliced

1 onion, chopped

2 garlic cloves, chopped

1/3 cup rice

1 can of diced tomatoes, undrained

2 cups of fresh spinach, cut

1 tbsp olive oil

4 cups vegetable broth

salt and pepper to taste

Directions:

Heat a large pot over medium heat. Add olive oil and onion and sauté for 2 minutes. Add leeks and cook for another 2-3 minutes, then add garlic and stir. Season with salt and pepper to taste.

Add the vegetable broth, canned tomatoes, and rice. Bring to a boil then reduce heat and simmer for about 10 minutes. Stir in spinach and cook for another 5 minutes

Vegetable Soup with Rice

Serves 6

Ingredients:

1 onion, chopped

1 potato, diced

1 carrot, diced

1 red bell pepper, chopped

2 tomatoes, chopped

1 zucchini, diced

1/3 cup rice

1 tsp dried oregano

3-4 tbsp olive oil

black pepper to taste

4 cups water

2 tbsp fresh lemon juice

Directions:

Heat the oil in a large soup pot and gently sauté the onions and carrot for 2-3 minutes stirring occasionally. Add in the potato, bell pepper, tomatoes, spices and water. Stir to combine.

Cover, bring to a boil then lower heat and simmer for 10 minutes. Add in the well washed rice and stir. Add the zucchini; cover and simmer for 15 minutes or until the vegetables are tender. Add in the lemon juice; stir to combine.

Broccoli and Potato Soup

Serves 6

Ingredients:

2 lbs broccoli, cut into florets

2 potatoes, chopped

1 big onion, chopped

3 garlic cloves, crushed

4 cups water

1 tbsp olive oil

1/4 tsp ground nutmeg

Directions:

Heat oil in a large saucepan over medium-high heat. Add onion and garlic and sauté, stirring, for 3 minutes or until soft.

Add broccoli, potato and four cups of cold water. Cover and bring to the boil then reduce heat to low. Simmer, stirring, for 10 to 15 minutes or until potato is tender. Remove from heat. Blend until smooth.

Return to pan. Cook for five minutes or until heated through. Season with nutmeg and pepper before serving.

Potato Soup

Serves 8

Ingredients:

4-5 medium potatoes, cut into small cubes

2 carrots, chopped

1 zucchini, chopped

1 celery rib, chopped

3 cups water

3 tbsp olive oil

1 cup whole milk

1/2 tsp dried rosemary

salt to taste

black pepper to taste

a bunch of fresh parsley for garnish, finely cut

Directions:

Heat the olive oil over medium heat and sauté the vegetables for 2-3 minutes. Pour 3 cups of water, add the rosemary and bring the soup to a boil, then lower heat and simmer until all the vegetables are tender.

Blend soup in a blender until smooth. Add a cup of warm milk and blend some more. Serve warm , seasoned with black pepper and parsley sprinkled over each serving.

Leek, Rice and Potato Soup

Serves 6

Ingredients:

1 small onion, finely cut

2 leeks, halved lengthwise and sliced

2-3 potatoes, diced

1/3 cup rice

4 cups of water

3 tbsp sunflower oil

lemon juice, to serve

Directions:

Heat a soup pot over medium heat. Add sunflower oil and onion and sauté for 2 minutes. Add leeks and potatoes and stir for a few minutes more.

Add 4 cups of water, bring to a boil, reduce heat and simmer for 5 minutes. Add the very well washed rice and simmer for 10 minutes. Serve with lemon juice to taste.

Carrot and Chickpea Soup

Serves 4-5

Ingredients:

3-4 big carrots, chopped

1 leek, chopped

4 cups vegetable broth

1 cup canned chick peas, undrained

1/2 cup orange juice

2 tbsp olive oil

1/2 tsp cumin

1/2 tsp ginger

4-5 tbsp yogurt, to serve

Directions:

Heat oil in a large saucepan over medium heat. Add leek and carrots and sauté until soft. Add orange juice, broth, chickpeas and spices.

Bring to the boil. Reduce heat to medium-low and simmer, covered, for 15 minutes. Blend soup until smooth, return to pan. Season with salt and pepper.

Stir over heat until heated through. Pour in 4-5 bowls, top with yogurt and serve.

Spicy Carrot Soup

Serves 6-7

Ingredients:

10 carrots, peeled and chopped

2 medium onions, chopped

4-5 cups water

5 tbsp olive oil

2 cloves garlic, minced

1 red chili pepper, finely chopped

1/2 bunch, fresh coriander, finely cut

salt and pepper to taste

1/2 cup heavy cream

Directions:

Heat the olive oil in a large pot over medium heat, and sauté the onions, carrots, garlic and chili pepper until tender. Add 4-5 cups of water and bring to a boil. Reduce heat to low, and simmer 30 minutes.

Transfer the soup to a blender or food processor and blend until smooth. Return to the pot, and continue cooking for a few more minutes. Remove soup from heat, and stir in the cream.

Serve with coriander sprinkled over each serving.

Lentil, Barley and Mushroom Soup

Serves 4

Ingredients:

2 medium leeks, trimmed, halved, sliced

10 white mushrooms, sliced

3 garlic cloves, cut

2 bay leaves

2 cans tomatoes, chopped, undrained

3/4 cup red lentils

1/3 cup barley

3 cups water

3 tbsp olive oil

1 tsp paprika

1 tsp savory

1/2 tsp cumin

Directions:

Heat oil in a large saucepan over medium-high heat. Sauté leeks and mushrooms for 3 to 4 minutes or until softened. Add cumin, paprika, savory and tomatoes, lentils, barley and 3 cups of cold water. Season with salt and pepper.

Cover and bring to the boil. Reduce heat to low. Simmer for 35-40 minutes or until barley is tender.

Mushroom Soup

Serves 4

Ingredients:

2 cups mushrooms, peeled and chopped

1 onion, chopped

2 cloves of garlic, crushed and chopped

1 tsp dried thyme

1 cup vegetable broth

salt and pepper to taste

3 tbsp sunflower or olive oil

Directions:

Sauté onions and garlic in a large soup pot until transparent. Add thyme and mushrooms.

Cook, stirring, for 10 minutes then add vegetable broth and simmer for another 10-20 minutes. Blend, season and serve.

French Vegetable Soup

Serves 6

Ingredients:

1 leek, thinly sliced

1 large zucchini, diced

1 cup green beans, cut

2 garlic cloves, cut

3 cups vegetable broth

1 can tomatoes, chopped

3.5 oz vermicelli, broken into small pieces

3 tbsp olive oil

black pepper to taste

4 tbsp freshly grated Parmesan cheese

Directions:

Heat olive oil in a large soup pot and sauté the leek, zucchini, green beans and garlic for about 5 minutes. Add the vegetable broth and stir in the tomatoes.

Bring to the boil, then reduce heat. Add black pepper to taste and simmer for 10 minutes or until the vegetables are tender, but still holding their shape.

Stir in the vermicelli. Cover again and simmer for 5 more minutes. Serve warm sprinkled with Parmesan cheese.

Minted Pea Soup

Serves 4

Ingredients:

1 onion, finely chopped

2 garlic cloves, finely chopped

3 cups vegetable broth

1/3 cup mint leaves

2 lb green peas, frozen

3 tbsp sunflower oil

1/4 cup yogurt, to serve

small mint leaves, to serve

Directions:

Heat oil in a large saucepan over medium-high heat and sauté onion and garlic for 5 minutes or until soft.

Add vegetable broth and bring to the boil then add mint and peas. Cover, reduce heat and cook for 10 minutes or until peas are tender but still green. Remove from heat.

Set aside to cool slightly then blend soup, in batches, until smooth. Return soup to saucepan over medium-low heat and cook until heated through. Season with salt and pepper. Serve topped with yogurt, pepper and mint leaves.

Italian Minestrone

Serves 6-7

Ingredients:

1/4 cabbage, chopped

2 carrots, chopped

1 celery rib, thinly sliced

1 small onion, chopped

2 garlic cloves, chopped

2 tbsp olive oil

2 cups water

1 can tomatoes, diced, undrained

1 cup fresh spinach, torn

1/2 cup pasta, cooked

black pepper and salt to taste

Directions:

Sauté carrots, cabbage, celery, onion and garlic in oil for 5 minutes in a deep saucepan. Add water, tomatoes and bring to a boil.

Reduce heat and simmer uncovered, for 20 minutes or until vegetables are tender. Stir in spinach, pasta and season with pepper and salt to taste.

Tomato Soup

Serves: 5-6

Ingredients:

4 cups chopped fresh tomatoes or 800 ml canned tomatoes

1 large onion, diced

4 garlic cloves, minced

3 tbsp olive or sunflower oil

1 cup hot water

1 tsp salt

1/2 tsp black pepper

1 tbsp sugar

1/2 bunch fresh parsley

Directions:

Sauté onions and garlic in oil in a large soup pot. When onions have softened, add tomatoes and cook until onions are golden and tomatoes soft. Stir in the spices and mix well to coat vegetables.

Add one cup of hot water. Blend the soup then return to the pot. Add a tbsp sugar and bring to boil, then simmer 20-30 minutes stirring occasionally. Sprinkle with parsley and serve

Cauliflower Soup

Serves 8

Ingredients:

1 large onion finely cut

1 medium head cauliflower, chopped

2-3 garlic cloves, minced

2 cups water

1/2 cup whole cream

4 tbsp olive oil

salt, to taste

fresh ground black pepper, to taste

Directions:

Heat the olive oil in a large pot over medium heat, and sauté the onion, cauliflower, garlic, Stir in the water, and bring the soup to a boil.

Reduce heat, cover, and simmer for 40 minutes. Remove the soup from heat add the cream and blend in a blender. Season with salt and pepper.

Roasted Red Pepper Soup

Serves 6-7

Ingredients:

5-6 red peppers

1 large onion, chopped

2 garlic cloves, crushed

4 medium tomatoes, chopped

2 cups vegetable broth

3 tbsp olive oil

2 bay leaves

Directions:

Grill the peppers or roast them in the oven at 480 F until the skins are a little burnt. Place the roasted peppers in a brown paper bag or a lidded container and leave covered for about 10 minutes. This makes it easier to peel them. Peel the skins and remove the seeds. Cut the peppers in small pieces.

Heat oil in a large saucepan over medium-high heat. Add onion and garlic and sauté, stirring, for 3 minutes or until onion has softened. Add the red peppers, bay leaves, tomato and simmer for 5 minutes.

Add broth. Season with pepper. Bring to the boil then reduce heat and simmer for 20 more minutes. Set aside to cool slightly. Blend, in batches, until smooth and serve.

Spinach Soup

Serves 6

Ingredients:

1 lb spinach, frozen

1 large onion or 4-5 spring onions

1 carrot

2 cups water

3-4 tbsp olive oil

1/4 cup white rice

1-2 cloves garlic, crushed

1 tsp paprika

black pepper

salt

Directions:

Chop the onion and spinach. Heat the oil in a cooking pot, add the onion and carrot and sauté together for a few minutes, until just softened. Add chopped garlic, paprika and rice and stir for a minute.

Remove from heat. Add the chopped spinach along with about 2 cups of hot water and season with salt and pepper. Bring back to a boil, then reduce the heat and simmer for around 15 minutes.

Spring Nettle Soup

Serves 6

Ingredients:

1.5 lb young top shoots of nettles, well washed

3-4 tbsp sunflower oil

2 potatoes, diced small

1 bunch spring onions, coarsely chopped

2 cups freshly boiled water

1 tsp salt

Directions:

Clean the young nettles, wash and cook them in slightly salted water. Drain, rinse, drain again and then chop or pass through a sieve.

Sauté the chopped spring onions and potatoes in the oil until the potatoes start to color a little. Turn off the heat, add the nettles, then gradually stir in the water. Stir well, then simmer until the potatoes are cooked through.

Gazpacho

Serves 6-7

Ingredients:

2.25 lb tomatoes, peeled and halved

1 onion, sliced

1 green pepper, sliced

1 big cucumber, peeled and sliced

2 cloves garlic

salt to taste

4 tbsp olive oil

1 tbsp apple vinegar

to garnish

1/2 onion, chopped

1 green pepper, chopped

1 cucumber, chopped

Directions:

Place the tomatoes, garlic, onion, green pepper, cucumber, salt, olive oil and vinegar in a blender or food processor and puree until smooth, adding small amounts of cold water if needed to achieve desired consistency.

Serve the gazpacho chilled with the chopped onion, green pepper and cucumber.

Cold Cucumber Soup

Serves 6

Ingredients:

1 large or two small cucumbers

2 cups yogurt

4-5 cloves garlic, crushed or chopped

1 cup cold water

4 tbsp sunflower or olive oil

2 bunches of fresh dill, finely chopped

1/2 cup crushed walnuts

Directions:

Wash the cucumber, peel and cut into small cubes. In a large bowl dilute the yogurt with water to taste, add the cucumber and garlic stirring well.

Add salt to the taste, garnish with the dill and the crushed walnuts and put in the fridge to cool.

Main Dishes

Bulgarian Beef Stew

Serves 6

Ingredients:

1.5 lb boneless beef chuck, cut into 1 1/2-inch cubes

2 onions, chopped

5 garlic cloves, minced

1 carrot, chopped

2 bay leaves

3 tbsp sunflower oil

1 tbsp paprika

1 tsp savory

1 cup beef broth

1/2 cup dry red wine

a bunch of parsley

2 tbsp tomato paste (optional)

salt

Directions:

Heat oil in a heavy large pot over medium heat. Pat dry and sprinkle meat with salt and pepper. Add to pot together with paprika and savory. Seal the meat, stirring from time to time, until it is well browned.

Add onions, garlic and bay leaves. Sauté until onions are golden, about five minutes. Add broth and wine. If you decide to use tomato paste, dilute it in the broth and add it this way.

Bring to a boil then reduce heat, cover and simmer until meat is very tender, stirring occasionally, about 1 hour 30 minutes.

When the meat is done, uncover the saucepan and allow the remaining water to evaporate.

Serve hot, sprinkled with parsley over rice or potato mash.

Sausage and Beans

Serves 4

Ingredients:

1.7 lb lean beef sausages

1 big onion, thinly sliced

2 garlic cloves, crushed

2 cups canned white beans, drained, rinsed

1 cup canned tomatoes, drained, diced

1 tsp paprika

1 tbsp mint

1 tbsp sunflower oil

1/2 cup finely cut parsley, to serve

Directions:

Heat a non-stick frying pan over medium heat. Cook sausages for 8 to 10 minutes or until browned. Set aside to cool slightly the transfer to a board and cut.

Heat oil and sauté onions, garlic and paprika for 3-4 minutes or until onion is soft. Add beans, tomatoes and mint. Return sausages to pan.

Bring to the boil then reduce heat and simmer, uncovered, stirring occasionally, for 15 minutes until sauce is thick. Serve into bowls sprinkled with fresh parsley.

Basic Beef Mince

Serves 8

Ingredients:

2 lbs ground beef

1 onion, finely chopped

1 celery rib, finely chopped

1 red bell pepper, deseeded, finely chopped

1 green bell pepper, deseeded, finely chopped

2 cups canned tomatoes, chopped

2 tbsp sunflower oil

1 tsp savory

Directions:

Heat oil in a frying pan over medium high heat. Add onion, celery, and red and green bell peppers. Cook for four minutes or until soft.

Add ground beef and cook, stirring with a spoon to break up mince, for 10 minutes or until browned. Add tomatoes, salt and pepper to taste.

Bring to the boil then reduce heat to medium. Simmer for 10 to 15 minutes or until thick.

Moussaka

Serves 4

Ingredients:

1 lb ground beef

1 celery rib, finely chopped

1 carrot, peeled, finely chopped

1 onion, finely chopped

2 garlic cloves, crushed

1 cup canned tomatoes, drained, diced

5 potatoes, cut into cubes

1/2 cup fresh parsley leaves, finely cut

3 tbsp sunflower oil

1 tsp savory

1 tsp paprika

2/3 cup yogurt

1 egg, lightly beaten

salt and freshly ground black pepper

Directions:

Heat half the oil in a large frying pan over medium-high heat. Add the ground meat and cook, stirring with a spoon to break up any lumps, for 5 minutes or until mince changes colour. Transfer to a large baking dish.

Heat the remaining oil in the same pan. Add the carrot, onion, garlic, parsley, paprika and savory and sauté, stirring, for 10 minutes or until vegetables soften. Transfer to the baking dish.

Wash, peel and cut into small 1/4 inch cubes the potatoes. Stir potatoes into the meat and the vegetable mixture.

Combine very well, add 1/2 cup of water, stir again and bake in a preheated to 180 C oven for 30 minutes or until potatoes are cooked through. In a small bowl mix together the yogurt and egg, pour and spread it evenly over the Moussaka.

Bake for 5 more minutes or until golden. Set aside for five minutes and serve.

Minced Meat and Rice Stuffed Peppers

Serves 6

Ingredients:

8 red or green bell peppers, cored and seeded

2 lbs ground beef

1/4 cup rice, washed and drained

1 onion, chopped

1 tomato, chopped

a bunch of fresh parsley, chopped

3 tbsp sunflower oil

1 tbsp paprika

Directions:

Heat the oil and sauté the onion for 2-3 minutes. Remove from heat. Add paprika, ground beef, rice, tomato, and season with salt and pepper.

Stuff each pepper with the mixture using a spoon. Every pepper should be 3/4 full.

Arrange the peppers in a deep oven proof dish and top up with warm water to half fill the dish. Cover and bake for about 40-50 minutes at 350 F.

Meatballs in Tomato Sauce

Serves 6

Ingredients:

1 lb ground veal

1 lb ground pork

2 onions, grated

1 carrot, chopped

2 garlic cloves, cut

3-4 white mushrooms, sliced

1 cup fresh white breadcrumbs

1/3 cup parsley leaves, finely chopped, for the meatballs

3 cups canned tomatoes, diced

1/2 cup chicken broth

1/2 cup parsley leaves, to serve

Directions:

Combine veal and pork mince, one onion, breadcrumbs, parsley and salt and pepper in a large bowl. Roll tablespoonfuls of mince mixture into balls. Place meatballs on a tray lined with baking paper. Cover and set aside.

Heat oil in a deep frying pan. Sauté finely cut onion, carrot and garlic for 2- 3 minutes, stirring. Add mushrooms and stir again. Add tomatoes and broth and bring slowly to the boil over medium heat.

Drop meatballs into tomato mixture. Reduce heat to low and simmer, uncovered, for 30 minutes or until meatballs are cooked through. Sprinkle with parsley, set aside for 5 minutes, and serve.

Mediterranean Meatloaf

Serves 4

Ingredients:

1/3 cup brown rice

1 small red onion, grated

1 lb ground beef

1 carrot, peeled, grated

3 oz feta cheese, crumbled

2 tbsp tomato sauce

1 egg, lightly beaten

2 tbsp basil leaves, finely cut

1 zucchini, thinly sliced

1 cup cherry tomatoes

1 garlic clove, crushed

2-3 tbsp olive oil

Directions:

Cook rice following package directions. Set aside to cool.

Preheat oven to 350 F. Grease base and sides of a 8 x 4 x 2.5 inch loaf pan or line it with baking paper, allowing a 1 inch overhang at both long ends.

Combine rice, onion, mince, carrot, feta, sauce, egg and basil in a bowl. Mix well and press into prepared pan. Place zucchini, tomatoes and garlic in a bowl. Toss in olive oil. Arrange over meatloaf.

Bake for 40-50 minutes or until meatloaf is firm. Set aside for 10 minutes, slice and serve.

Bulgarian Pork and Rice Stew

Serves 4

Ingredients:

1.5 lb pork cubed (leg or neck)

1 onion, cut

2 cups rice, washed

6 cups water

4 tbsp sunflower oil

1/2 cup finely cut parsley leaves, to serve

Directions:

Cut pork into cubes. Heat two tbsp of oil in a large, deep, frying pan over medium-high heat. Cook pork, turning, for 4-5 minutes or until browned. Transfer to an oven proof baking dish.

In the same pan, heat the remaining oil and sauté onion for 2-3 minutes. Add washed and drained rice and cook for 2-3 minutes, stirring, until transparent. Transfer rice to the baking dish.

Add 6 cups of warm water, stir well and bake in a preheated to 350 F oven for 40 minutes, stirring half way through. When ready, sprinkle with parsley, set aside for 2-3 minutes and serve.

Chicken Potato Casserole

Serves 4

Ingredients:

4 skinless, boneless chicken breast halves

12 oz baby potatoes

1 onion, sliced

2 carrots, cut

1 red bell pepper, halved, deseeded, cut

1 zucchini, cut

4 garlic cloves, thinly sliced

1 cup water

3 tbsp olive oil

1 tsp dry oregano

Directions:

Preheat oven to 350 F. Heat oil in a non stick frying pan over medium heat. Cook half the chicken, turning occasionally, for 5 minutes or until brown all over. Set aside. Repeat with remaining chicken.

Peel the potatoes and cut into quarters, lengthwise. Peel and cut the carrots and the zucchini. Cut the onion and the pepper. Transfer chicken to a roasting pan, add vegetables, on and around the chicken. Add dry oregano, garlic and water, distributing evenly across the pan.

Roast uncovered at 350 F for one hour. Half way through stir gently. If needed, add a little more water.

Chicken and Onion Stew

Serves 4

Ingredients:

4 chicken breast halves

4-5 big onions, thinly sliced

1/2 cup black olives, pitted

4 tbsp olive oil

1 tsp thyme

1 tsp turmeric

salt and black pepper to taste

1/4 cup parsley leaves, chopped, to serve

Directions:

Heat the oil in a large, deep, frying pan over medium-high heat. Cook chicken, turning, for 4 to 5 minutes or until golden. Transfer to a plate.

Sauté thinly sliced onions, stirring gently, for 5 minutes until soft. Add olives, thyme, turmeric, salt and pepper to taste. Return chicken to pan.

Cover and bring to the boil. Reduce heat to low and simmer for 35 minutes or until chicken is cooked through. Sprinkle with parsley and serve.

Chicken and Mushroom Stew

Serves 4

Ingredients:

4 chicken breast halves, cut into bite size pieces

1 lb mushrooms, sliced (5-6 cups)

1 bunch of spring onions, chopped

1/2 cup light cream

4 tbsp olive oil

1 tsp thyme

salt and black pepper to taste

Directions:

Heat oil in a large, deep, frying pan over medium high heat. Cook chicken, stirring, for 4-5 minutes or until golden. Add spring onions, mushrooms, salt and pepper and stir.

Cover and bring to the boil. Reduce heat to low and simmer for 20 minutes then stir in cream. Simmer for 5 more minutes and serve.

Mediterranean Chicken Drumstick Casserole

Serves 4

Ingredients:

8 chicken drumsticks

1 leek, trimmed, thinly sliced

2 garlic cloves, crushed

1 cup canned tomatoes

1 tsp dry rosemary

1 cup canned chickpeas, drained and rinsed

cooked orzo or couscous, to serve

Directions:

Preheat oven to 350 F. Heat the oil in a non stick frying pan over medium heat. Add half the chicken and cook, turning occasionally, for 5 minutes or until brown all over. Transfer chicken to a big baking dish. Repeat with the remaining chicken.

Add leek and garlic to the pan and cook, stirring, for 3 minutes or until soft. Add tomatoes, chick peas, thyme and rosemary, and bring to the boil. Remove from heat. Pour over the chicken.

Cover and bake for 40 minutes or until chicken is tender. Season with salt and pepper. Serve with orzo or couscous.

Greek Chicken Casserole

Serves 4

Ingredients:

4 skinless, boneless chicken breast halves or 8 tights

2 lb potatoes, cubed

1/2 lb green beans, trimmed and cut in 1 inch pieces

1 big onion, chopped

2 cups diced, canned tomatoes, undrained

5 garlic cloves, crushed

1/4 cup water

1/2 cup feta cheese, crumbled

salt and black pepper to taste

Directions:

Preheat oven to 350 F. Heat oil in a large baking dish over medium heat. Add onion and sauté for 2 minutes. Add thyme, black pepper and garlic and sauté for another minute. Add potatoes and sauté for 2-3 minutes or until they begin to brown. Stir in beans, water, and tomatoes.

Remove from heat. Arrange chicken pieces into the vegetables, sprinkle with salt and pepper and top with feta.

Cover and bake for 40 minutes, stirring gently halfway through. Serve the vegetable mixture onto a plate, underneath or beside the chicken.

Hunter Style Chicken

Serves 4-6

Ingredients:

1 chicken (3-4 lbs), cut into pieces

2 tbsp olive or sunflower oil

2 medium onions, thinly sliced

1 red bell pepper, cut

6-7 white mushrooms, sliced

2 cups canned tomatoes, diced and drained

3 garlic cloves, thinly sliced

salt and freshly ground pepper

1/3 cup white wine

1/2 cup parsley leaves, finely cut

1 tsp sugar

Directions:

Rinse chicken pieces and pat dry. Heat olive oil in a large skillet on medium heat. Working in batches cook the chicken pieces until nicely browned, 5-6 minutes, then turn over and brown the other side.

Transfer chicken to a bowl, set aside. Drain off all of the rendered fat. Add 2 tbsp of olive oil and sauté the sliced onions and bell pepper for a few minutes. Add the mushrooms and cook some more until onion is translucent. Add garlic and cook a minute more.

Add wine and simmer until liquid is reduced by half. Add tomatoes and a tsp of sugar and stir. Place the chicken pieces on top of the tomatoes and onions, skin side up.

Lower the heat and cover the skillet with the lid slightly ajar. Simmer the chicken for about 40 minutes, turning from time to time, until meat is almost falling off the bones.

Sprinkle with parsley, set aside for 3-4 minutes and serve.

Chicken Kofta

Serves 4

Ingredients:

1 lb ground chicken meat

1 onion, grated

1 egg, lightly whisked

1/3 cup breadcrumbs

3 tbsp chopped parsley leaves

1 tbs freshly ground ginger

1/2 tsp ground cinnamon

1/2 tsp ground nutmeg

2 tbsp olive oil

1 cup chicken broth

1 tsp brown sugar

1 tbsp lemon juice

Directions:

Preheat the oven to 350 F. Line a baking tray with baking paper.

Place the ground chicken, onion, egg, breadcrumbs, chopped parsley, cinnamon, nutmeg and half the ginger in a bowl with a tsp salt. Mix with your hands until well combined. Using damp hands, roll mixture into walnut-sized balls, then place them on a tray in a single layer and bake for 15 minutes until light golden.

Heat oil in a deep frying pan over medium heat. Add remaining ginger and stir for 1 minute until fragrant. Add tomatoes and cook for 2 minutes. Add broth and sugar.

Bring to a boil, then reduce heat to medium low and simmer for 5 minutes.

Add kofta and simmer for 20 minutes until kofta are cooked through and sauce has thickened. Serve kofta with rice, orzo or couscous garnished with extra parsley.

Grilled Chicken with Sumac

Serves 4

Ingredients:

1 whole chicken (3-4 lbs)

2 tbsp olive oil

2 garlic cloves, crushed

1 tbsp sumac

1 tsp lemon zest

1 tbsp lemon juice

1/2 cup fresh coriander leaves

Directions:

Wash chicken and pat dry with paper towel.

Combine oil, garlic, sumac, lemon rind and lemon juice in a bowl. Rub mixture over chicken. Cover and marinate for 2 hours if time permits. Bake chicken in an oven proof dish, covered, for 1 1/2 hours.

Uncover and bake for 20 minutes more or until cooked through. Cut chicken into large pieces and serve sprinkled with coriander and garnished with vegetable salads.

Chicken Skewers

Serves 4

Ingredients:

1.5 lb chicken breast fillets, cut in bite size pieces

3-4 tbsp sunflower oil

2 garlic cloves, crushed

1 tsp paprika

1 tsp dried savory

Directions:

Thread chicken pieces onto skewers. Place in a shallow dish. Combine sunflower oil and lemon juice, garlic, paprika and savory. Pour over chicken. Turn to coat. Marinate for 40 minutes, if time permits.

Preheat barbecue on medium high heat. Cook skewers for 3-4 minutes each side or until chicken is just cooked through. Serve with vegetable salad.

Moroccan Chicken Tagine

Serves 4-5

Ingredients:

1 whole chicken (3-4 lbs), cut into pieces

2 large onions, grated

2 or 3 cloves of garlic, finely chopped or pressed

1 tsp ginger

1 tsp cumin

1 tsp paprika

1 tsp black pepper

1 tsp turmeric

1/2 tsp salt

1/2 cup green or black olives, or mixed

1 preserved lemon, quartered and deseeded

5 tbsp olive oil

one bunch of fresh coriander

one bunch of fresh parsley

Directions:

Rinse and dry chicken and place onto a clean plate.

In a large bowl, mix three tablespoons of olive oil, salt, half the onions, garlic, ginger, cumin, paprika, and turmeric. Mix thoroughly, crush the garlic with your fingers, and add a little water to make a paste.

Roll the chicken pieces into the marinade and leave for 10 to 15 minutes.

Heat the tagine base on medium heat and add 2 tablespoons of olive oil. Add the chicken and pour excess marinade juices over the top. Add the remaining onions, olives, and chopped preserved lemon. Tie the parsley and coriander together into a bouquet and place on top of the chicken.

Place the lid on the base, bring to a boil, and immediately reduce to a simmer. Cook for 45 minutes or until the chicken is cooked through and quite tender. Serve with couscous, rice, or rice pilaf.

Mediterranean Chicken Couscous

Serves 6

Ingredients:

2 chicken breast halves, cut into strips

2 garlic cloves, finely chopped

1 tbsp freshly ground black pepper

1 cup chicken broth

1 lemon, rind finely grated, juiced

2 cups couscous

1 cup cherry tomatoes, halved

1/2 cup green olives, pitted, halved

1/2 cup fresh parsley leaves, chopped

5-6 spring onions, trimmed, chopped

2 tbs drained capers, chopped

3 tbsp olive oil

Directions:

Marinate the chicken in the oil, garlic and black pepper in a shallow dish. Heat a large saucepan over medium high heat. Add half the chicken mixture and cook for 2-3 minutes, tossing, until just cooked. Transfer to a plate, cover loosely with foil to keep warm and set aside. Repeat with the remaining chicken mixture.

Increase heat to high and add broth and lemon juice to the pan. Cook, until the liquid comes to the boil. Remove from the heat and add the couscous. Cover and set aside for 2-3 minutes or until all the liquid is absorbed. Use a fork to fluff the grains.

Add the chicken, lemon rind, tomatoes, olives, parsley, spring onions and capers. Toss well to combine.

Chicken with Rice

Serves 6

Ingredients:

1 chicken 2-3 lbs, cut into serving pieces, or 2-3 lbs chicken thighs or breasts, rinsed and patted dry

5 tablespoons olive oil

1 medium onion, chopped

1 carrot, chopped

1 garlic clove, minced

2 cups white rice

2 cups chicken broth

1 cup water

1 cup of diced fresh or cooked tomatoes, strained

1 tsp savory

1 tsp salt

freshly ground black pepper, to taste

Directions:

Heat 3 tbsp olive oil in a large skillet on medium high heat. Cook chicken pieces a few minutes on each side, enough to seal them. Remove from pan and set aside.

In the same pan, heat the remaining olive oil and sauté the onions, garlic and carrot for 2-3 minutes. Add the rice and cook it stirring until transparent.

Transfer rice mixture to a baking dish. Pour over the chicken broth, tomatoes and water. Stir until well combined. Arrange chicken pieces on top, skin side up, and bake in a preheated to 350 F oven for 30-40 minutes until the rice and chicken are done.

Chicken Moussaka

Serves 6

Ingredients:

2 big eggplants, cut into 1/2 inch thick rounds

olive oil cooking spray

1 tbsp salt

1 big onion, chopped

1/2 tsp ground cinnamon

1/2 tsp ground nutmeg

1/4 tsp ground coriander

1/4 tsp ground ginger

2 cups canned tomatoes, undrained, chopped

2 cups skinless roast chicken, shredded

1/2 cup finely chopped fresh parsley leaves

1 tsp sugar

1 cup yogurt

1 cup Parmesan cheese

salt and black pepper to taste

Directions:

Place eggplant slices on a tray and sprinkle with plenty of salt. Let sit for 30 minutes, then rinse with cold water. Lay slices out flat and use a clean kitchen towel to squeeze out excess water and pat dry.

Heat a frying pan over medium high heat. Spray both sides of eggplant with oil. Cook, in batches, for 3 to 4 minutes each side or until golden. Transfer to a plate.

In the same pan sauté onion, stirring, for 3 to 4 minutes or until softened. Add spice and sauté for one minute until fragrant. Add tomatoes and sugar, stir and cook until thickened. Add chicken and parsley and stir well to combine.

Arrange half the eggplant slices in a baking dish. Cover with chicken and tomato mixture and arrange remaining eggplant. Top with yogurt and sprinkle with Parmesan cheese. Bake for 30 minutes or until golden. Set aside for five minutes and serve.

Artichoke and Onion Frittata

Serves 4

Ingredients:

1 small onion, chopped

1 cup marinated artichoke hearts, drained

6 eggs

1 garlic clove, crushed

1 tbsp olive oil

salt and freshly ground black pepper

1/2 bunch fresh parsley, finely cut, to serve

Directions:

Heat oil in a non-stick oven pan over medium heat and sauté onion stirring occasionally, for 5-6 minutes or until golden brown. Add artichokes and cook for 2 minutes or until heated through.

Whisk eggs with garlic until combined well. Season with salt and pepper. Pour the egg mixture over the artichoke mixture. Reduce heat, cover and cook for 10 minutes or until frittata is set around the edge but still runny in the center.

Place pan into preheated oven and cook 4-5 until golden brown. Remove from oven and cut into wedges. Serve sprinkled with parsley.

Feta Cheese Stuffed Zucchinis

Serves 5-6

Ingredients:

5-6 zucchinis

3.5 oz feta cheese, grated

3 eggs

1 onion, finely chopped

1/2 cup milk

3.5 oz butter

salt

Directions:

Halve the peeled zucchinis lengthwise, hollow and salt. Sauté the finely chopped onion in half of the butter. Combine half of the milk, grated feta cheese and 1 egg in a bowl.

Stuff the zucchinis with the mixture, arrange in a baking dish and pour over the remaining 2 eggs beaten with the rest of the milk.

Bake for approximately 30 min in a preheated oven. A few minutes before the dish is ready fleck the remaining butter over the zucchinis.

Zucchini and Almond Pasta

Serves 4

Ingredients:

2 cups fusilli (or other short pasta)

1 tbsp olive oil

2 garlic cloves, crushed

4 zucchinis, coarsely grated

1/2 cup slivered almonds, lightly toasted

2 tbs chopped fresh parsley

1 tbs chopped mint leaves

2 tbs grated Parmesan cheese

Directions:

Cook the pasta according to package instructions until al dente.

Heat oil in a large frying pan over medium heat and sauté the garlic and for 30 seconds. Add the zucchinis and sauté, stirring occasionally, for 5 minutes or until all the liquid has evaporated. Add almonds and herbs, stir to combine and season with salt and pepper.

Drain the cooked pasta, add to the pan together with the Parmesan and toss to combine.

Poached Eggs with Feta and Yogurt

Serves 4

Ingredients:

12 eggs

2 cups plain yogurt

10 oz feta cheese, shredded

2 tsp paprika

3 cloves garlic

2 oz butter

Directions:

Crush the garlic and stir together with the yogurt and the grated cheese. Divide the mixture into four plates.

Poach the eggs, take them out with a serving spoon and place three eggs on top of the mixture in each plate.

Brown the butter together with the red pepper and pour one quarter over each plate before serving.

Mish-Mash

Serves 5-6

Ingredients:

2 small onions, chopped

1 green bell pepper, chopped

2 red bell peppers, chopped

4 tomatoes, cubed

2 garlic cloves, crushed

8 eggs

9 oz feta cheese, crumbled

4 tbsp olive oil

half a bunch parsley

black pepper

salt

Directions:

In a large pan sauté onions over medium heat, till transparent. Reduce heat and add bell peppers and garlic. Continue cooking until soft.

Add the tomatoes and continue simmering until the mixture is almost dry. Add the cheese and all eggs and cook until well mixed and not too liquid.

Season with black pepper and remove from heat. Sprinkle with parsley.

Eggs and Feta Cheese Stuffed Peppers

Serves 4

Ingredients:

8 red bell peppers

6 eggs

4 oz feta cheese

a bunch of parsley

2 cups breadcrumbs

sunflower oil

Directions:

Grill the peppers or roast them in the oven at 480 F. Peel and deseed the peppers.

Mix the crumbled feta cheese with 4 beaten eggs. Stuff the peppers with the mixture. Beat the remaining two eggs.

Roll each stuffed pepper first in breadcrumbs then dip in the beaten eggs. Fry in hot oil turning once. Serve sprinkled with parsley.

Feta Cheese Baked in Foil

Serves 4

Ingredients:

14 oz hard feta cheese

3 oz butter

1 tbsp paprika

1 tsp savory

Directions:

Cut the feta cheese into four medium-thick slices and place on sheets of butter-lined foil.

Place cubes of butter on top each feta cheese piece, sprinkle with paprika and savory and wrap. Place in a tray and bake in a moderate oven. Serve wrapped in the foil.

Breaded Cheese

Serves 4

Ingredients:

14 oz feta cheese

2 eggs, beaten

2 tbsp flour

3-4 tbsp bread crumbs

vegetable oil for frying

Directions:

Cut the cheese in four equal slices. Dip each piece first in cold water, then roll in the flour, then in the beaten eggs, and finally in the breadcrumbs.

Fry these cheese pieces in preheated oil on both sides. Serve warm.

Bulgarian Baked Beans

Serves 6

Ingredients:

2 cups dried white beans

2 medium onions, chopped

1 red bell pepper, chopped

1 carrot, chopped

1/4 cup sunflower oil

1 tsp paprika

1 tsp black pepper

1 tbsp plain flour

1/2 bunch fresh parsley and mint

1 tsp salt

Directions:

Wash the beans and soak in water overnight. In the morning discard the water, pour enough cold water to cover the beans, add one of the onions, peeled but left whole.

Cook until the beans are soft but not falling apart. If there is too much water left, drain the beans.

Chop the other onion and fry it a frying pan along with the chopped bell pepper and the carrot. Add paprika, plain flour and the beans. Stir well and pour the mixture in a baking dish along with some parsley, mint, and salt.

Bake in a preheated to 350 F oven for 20-30 minutes. The beans should not be too dry. Serve warm.

Rice Stuffed Bell Peppers

Serves 4

Ingredients:

8 bell peppers, cored and seeded

1 1/2 cups rice, washed and drained

2 onions, chopped

1 tomato, chopped

fresh parsley, chopped

3 tbsp oil

1 tbsp paprika

Directions:

Heat the oil and sauté the onions for 2-3 minutes. Add the paprika, the washed and rinsed rice, the tomato, and season with salt and pepper. Add 1/2 cup of hot water and cook the rice until the water is absorbed.

Stuff each pepper with the mixture using a spoon. Every pepper should be 3/4 full. Arrange the peppers in a deep oven proof dish and top up with warm water to half fill the dish.

Cover and bake for about 20 minutes at 350 F. Uncover and cook for another 15 minutes until the peppers are well cooked. Serve on their own or with plain yogurt.

Beans Stuffed Bell Peppers

Serves 5

Ingredients:

10 dried red bell peppers

1 cup dried beans

1 onion

3 cloves garlic

2 tbsp flour

1 carrot

1 bunch of parsley

1/2 crushed walnuts

paprika

Salt

Directions:

Put the dried peppers in warm water and leave them for 1 hour. Cook the beans.

Chop the carrot and the onion, sauté them and add them to the cooked beans. Add as well the finely chopped parsley and the walnuts. Stir the mixture to make it homogeneous.

Drain the peppers, then fill them with the mixture and place in a roasting tin, covering the pepper's openings with flour to seal them during the baking. Bake it for about 30 min at 350 F.

Monastery Stew

Serves 4

Ingredients:

3-4 potatoes, diced

2-3 tomatoes, diced

1-2 carrots, chopped

1-2 onions, finely chopped

1 cup small shallots, whole

1 celery rib, chopped

2 cups fresh mushrooms, chopped

1/2 cup black olives, pitted

1/4 cup rice

1/2 cup white wine

1/2 cup sunflower oil

1 bunch of parsley

1 tsp black pepper

1 tsp salt

Directions:

Sauté the finely chopped onions, carrots and celery in a little oil. Add the small onions, olives, mushrooms and black pepper and stir well. Pour over the wine and 1 cup of water, salt, cover and let simmer until tender.

After 15 minutes add the diced potatoes, the rice, and the tomato pieces. Transfer everything into a clay pot, sprinkle with parsley and bake for about 30 minutes at 350 F.

Potato and Leek Stew

Serves 4

Ingredients:

3-4 potatoes

2-3 leek stems cut into thick rings

5-6 tbsp olive oil

1/2 bunch of parsley

1/2 cup grated yellow cheese (cheddar or Gruyère)

salt

Directions:

Peel the potatoes, wash them and cut them into small cubes. Slice the leeks. Put the potatoes and the leeks in a pot along with some water and the oil. The water should cover the vegetables.

Season with salt and bring to the boil then simmer until tender. Sprinkle with the finely chopped parsley and the grated yellow cheese.

Spinach with Rice

Serves 4

Ingredients:

3-4 cups fresh spinach, washed, drained and chopped

1/2 cup of rice

1 onion, chopped

1 carrot, chopped

1/4 cup olive oil

2 cups water

Directions:

Heat the oil in a large skillet and cook the onions and the carrot until soft, add the paprika and the washed and drained rice and mix well.

Add two cups of warm water stirring constantly as the rice absorbs it, and simmer for 10 more minutes.

Wash the spinach well and cut it in strips then add to the rice and cook until it wilts. Remove from the heat and season to taste. Serve with yogurt.

Stewed Green Beans

Serves 5-6

Ingredients:

2 lb green beans, fresh or frozen

2 onions, chopped

4 cloves garlic, crushed

1/2 cup sunflower oil

1 bunch fresh parsley, chopped

1 bunch of fresh dill, finely chopped

2 potatoes, peeled and cut in small chunks

2 carrots, sliced

1 cup water

2 tbsp salt

pepper to taste

Directions:

Sauté the onions and the garlic lightly in olive oil. Add the green beans, and the remaining ingredients.

Cover and simmer over medium heat for about an hour or until all vegetables are tender. Check after 30 minutes; add more water if necessary. Serve warm - sprinkled with the fresh dill.

Cabbage and Rice Stew

Serves 4

Ingredients:

1 cup long grain white rice

2 cups water

2 tbsp olive oil

1 small onion, chopped

1 clove garlic, crushed

1/4 head cabbage, cored and shredded

2 tomatoes, diced

1 tbsp paprika

1/2 bunch of parsley

salt to taste

black pepper to taste

Directions:

Heat the olive oil in a large pot. Add the onion and garlic and cook until transparent. Add the paprika, rice and water, stir and bring to boil.

Simmer for 10 minutes. Add the shredded cabbage, the tomatoes, and cook for about 20 minutes, stirring occasionally, until the cabbage cooks down.

Season with salt and pepper and serve sprinkled with parsley.

Potatoes Baked in Milk

Serves 5-6

Ingredients:

4-5 medium potatoes

1 cup milk

5 tbsp olive oil

1 tsp salt

1 tsp black pepper

1 tsp paprika

1 tsp savory

Directions:

Wash the potatoes, peel them and cut them in thin slices. Put in a large baking dish together with the milk, oil, salt, pepper, paprika and savory.

Mix everything very well. Bake for about 30 minutes at 350 F.

New Potatoes with Herbs

Serves 4-5

Ingredients:

2 lb small new potatoes

1 tbsp peppermint

2 oz butter

1 tbsp finely chopped parsley

1 tbsp rosemary

1 tbsp oregano

1 tbsp dill

1 tsp salt

1 tsp black pepper

Directions:

Wash the young potatoes, cut them in halves if too big, and put them in a baking dish.

Melt the butter and pour over the potatoes. Season with the herbs, salt and pepper. Bake for 30-40 minutes at 350 F

Breakfasts and Desserts

Strawberry Jam Crêpes

Serves 15

Ingredients:

3 eggs

1/4 cup sugar

2 cups plain flour

2 cups milk

1/2 orange, juiced

1/2 tsp vanilla

1/4 cup sunflower oil

1/2 cup strawberry jam

Directions:

Using an electric mixer, lightly beat eggs and sugar until well combined. Add 1/2 cup flour, 1 tablespoon at a time, beating well after each addition. Slowly add remaining 1 1/2 cups flour and milk alternately until batter is smooth. Reduce mixer speed. Add orange juice, vanilla and a pinch of salt. Beat until batter is smooth.

Heat a 7 inch base crêpe pan or frying pan over medium heat. Brush pan with a little oil. Pour 2 1/2 tablespoon of batter into center of pan and swirl to coat base. Cook for 1 to 2 minutes or until base is golden. Turn and cook for 30 seconds. Transfer to a plate. Repeat with remaining batter, greasing pan between crêpes.

Spread 1 teaspoon jam over 1 crêpe. Roll crêpe up tightly. Repeat with remaining crêpes and jam. Layer crêpes on a serving plate. Serve sprinkled with powdered sugar.

Fried Bread Slices

Serves 4

Ingredients:

8 slices stale bread

4 eggs, beaten

2/3 cup milk

1/2 cup sunflower oil

Directions:

Slice the bread into thin 1/2 inch slices. Dip first in milk, then in the beaten eggs.

Fry in hot oil. Serve hot, sprinkled with sugar, honey, jam, feta cheese or whatever topping you prefer.

Cinnamon Toast

Serves 4

Ingredients:

4 slices of sliced bread

4 tsp butter, softened or room temp

1 tsp cinnamon

2 tbsp sugar

Directions:

In a small bowl, mix very well cinnamon and sugar. Toast 4 bread slices. Spread butter on the toast.

Sprinkle the cinnamon sugar over the buttered toast and serve.

Quick Peach Tarts

Serves 4

Ingredients:

1 sheet frozen ready-rolled puff pastry

1/4 cup light cream cheese spread

2 tablespoons sugar

a pinch of cinnamon

4 peaches, peeled, halved, stones removed, sliced

Directions:

Line a baking tray with baking paper. Cut the pastry into 4 squares and place them on the prepared tray.

Using a spoon, mix cream cheese, sugar, vanilla and cinnamon. Spread over pastry squares. Arrange peach slices on top.

Bake in a preheated to 350 F oven for 10 minutes, or until golden.

Baked Apples

Serves 4

Ingredients:

8 medium sized apples

1/3 cup walnuts, crushed

3/4 cup sugar

3 tbsp raisins, soaked

vanilla, cinnamon according to taste

2 oz butter

Directions:

Peel and carefully hollow the apples. Prepare stuffing by combining the butter with sugar, crushed walnuts, raisins and cinnamon.

Stuff the apples with this mixture and place them in an oiled dish. Pour over 1-2 tablespoons of water and bake in a moderate oven. Serve warm with a scoop of vanilla ice cream.

Cherry Clafoutis

Serves 4

Ingredients:

1/2 cup flour

1/4 cup plus 2 tablespoons sugar

a pinch of salt

3 large eggs

3 tbsp unsalted butter, melted

zest of 1 lemon

1/4 cup plus 2 tbsp milk

3 cups cherries, pitted

1 tbsp Cognac or brandy (optional)

1 tsp vanilla extract

powdered sugar, for dusting

Directions:

Pit the cherries using a cherry pitter. Place then on a small tray in a single layer, sprinkle with 1/4 cup sugar and shake gently to coat. Place in the freezer for 1 hour or until firm.

Preheat the oven to 350 F. Butter a 9-inch gratin dish. In a bowl, whisk the flour, sugar, vanilla and a pinch of salt. Whisk in the eggs, melted butter, brandy and lemon zest. Beat until smooth. Add in the milk and continue whisking for about 3 minutes, until light and very smooth. Pour the batter into the dish and top with the cherries.

Bake for about 30 minutes, until the clafoutis is set and golden. Let cool slightly. Dust with powdered sugar.

Pumpkin Pastry

Serves 8

Ingredients:

14 oz filo pastry

1 cups pumpkin, shredded

1 cup walnuts, coarsely chopped

1/2 cup sugar

6 tbsp sunflower oil

1 tbsp cinnamon

1 tsp vanilla powder

1/2 cup powdered sugar, for dusting

Directions:

Grate the pumpkin and steam it until tender. Cool and add the walnuts, sugar, cinnamon and the vanilla.

Place a few sheets of pastry in the baking dish, sprinkle with oil and spread the filling on top. Repeat this a few times finishing with a sheet of pastry. Bake for 20 minutes at 350 F.

Let the Pumpkin Pie cool down and dust with the powdered sugar.

Sweet Cheese Balls with Syrup

Serves 6

Ingredients:

3.5 oz feta or cottage cheese

3 eggs

1 cup flour

1 tsp baking soda

1 cup sunflower oil

for the syrup:

1 1/2 cups sugar

1 1/2 cups water

juice of half a lemon

Directions:

Put water and sugar in a pot and bring to a boil, stirring. Boil it for about 4-5 minutes, then add the lemon juice. Continue boiling for 2-3 minutes, then set aside to cool.

Mix the feta cheese with the eggs, then gradually add the flour and the baking soda. Shape dough into balls with a spoon and fry in hot sunflower oil until golden-brown. Arrange cheese balls in a plate and pour over them the already cooled syrup

Bulgarian Cake

Serves 24

Ingredients:

3 eggs, beaten

1 cup sugar

1 cup yogurt

1/2 cup vegetable oil

1 tbsp baking powder

1 tbsp vanilla powder

1 tsp grated lemon rind

1 tbsp cocoa powder

3 cups flour

Directions:

Beat the eggs with the sugar and add the vegetable oil. Add in yogurt. Mix the baking powder with the flour and add it to the egg mixture along with vanilla and lemon rind.

Preheat the oven to 350 F and warm a 10 inch tube pan. Pour two thirds of the mixture into it. Add a tablespoon of cocoa powder to the remaining dough, mix well and pour it in the cake tin.

Bake for about 35 minutes or until a toothpick comes out clean.

Oatmeal Muffins

Serves 6

Ingredients:

1 cup rolled oats

1 cup flour

1/2 cup sugar

1/2 tsp salt

1 tsp baking powder

1/2 tsp baking soda

1/2 tsp of cinnamon

1/4 cup walnuts, crushed

1/3 cup raisins

1/2 cup butter, melted and cooled

1 cup buttermilk

1 tsp lemon zest

1 tsp vanilla extract

1 large egg, beaten

Directions:

Preheat the oven to 350 F and grease a twelve-hole muffin tin.

Mix together the oats, sugar, flour, salt, baking soda, baking powder, cinnamon, walnuts and raisins. In a separate bowl mix together the butter, buttermilk, egg, vanilla and lemon zest.

Pour the wet ingredients into the dry mixture and stir for about 15 seconds, just to bring the ingredients together. Scoop into the muffin tin and bake for 15 minutes or until a toothpick comes out clean. Set aside for a minute or two and transfer to a wire rack to cool completely.

Chocolate Peanut Butter Melts

Serves 24

Ingredients:

1 1/2 sheets frozen ready-rolled shortcrust pastry

1/2 cup smooth peanut butter

24 chocolate melts

Directions:

Preheat oven to 350 F. Grease two 12 hole mini muffin pans. Using a small cup cut 24 rounds from the pastry sheets. Press these rounds into the prepared pan holes. Spoon 1 teaspoon of peanut butter into each pastry case.

Bake for 8 minutes or until pastry is golden. Top each tart with one chocolate melt. Bake for two minutes more, or until the chocolate has melted. Transfer to a wire rack to cool slightly and serve.

Caramel Cream

Serves 8

Ingredients:

11/2 cup sugar

4 cups cold milk

8 eggs

2 tsp vanilla powder

Directions:

Melt 1/4 of the sugar in a non-stick pan over low heat. When the sugar has turned into caramel, pour it into 8 cup-sized ovenproof pots covering only the bottoms.

Whisk the eggs with the rest of the sugar and the vanilla, and slowly add the milk. Stir the mixture well and divide between the pots.

Place the 8 pots in a larger, deep baking dish. Pour 3-4 cups of water into the dish. Place the baking dish in a preheated to 280 F oven for about an hour and bake but do not let the water boil, as the boiling will overcook the cream and make holes in it: if necessary, add cold water or a few ice cubes to the baking dish.

Remove the baking dish from the oven; remove the pots from the dish. Place a shallow serving plate on top, then Invert each pot so that the cream unmolds. The caramel will form a topping and sauce.

Bulgarian Rice Pudding

Serves 4

Ingredients:

1 cup short-grain white rice

6 tbsp sugar

1 1/2 cup water

1 1/2 cup whole milk

1 cinnamon stick

1 strip lemon zest

Directions:

Place the rice in a saucepan, cover with water and cook over low heat for about 15 minutes. Add milk, sugar, cinnamon stick and lemon zest and cook over very low heat, stirring frequently until the mixture is creamy. Do not let it boil.

When ready, discard the cinnamon stick and lemon zest. Serve warm or at room temperature.

Baklava - Walnut Pie

Serves 15

Ingredients:

14 oz filo pastry

1 cup ground walnuts

9 oz butter

For the syrup:

2 cups sugar

2 cups water

1 tbsp vanilla powder

2 tbsp lemon zest

Directions:

Grease a baking tray and place 2-3 sheets of filo pastry. Crush the walnuts and spread some evenly on the pastry. Place two more sheets of the filo pastry on top. Repeat until all the pastry sheets and walnuts have been used up. Always finish with some sheets of pastry on top.

Cut the pie in the tray into small squares. Melt the butter and pour it over the pie.

Bake in a preheated oven at 390 F until light brown. When ready set aside to cool.

the syrup: Combine water and sugar in a saucepan. Add vanilla and lemon zest and bring to the boil, then lower the heat and simmer for about 5 minutes until the syrup is nearly thick.

Pour hot syrup over the cold baked pie, set aside for at least 1-2 days until the syrup is completely absorbed.

FREE BONUS RECIPES: 10 Natural Homemade Body Scrubs and Beauty Recipes

Dry Skin Body Scrub

Ingredients:

½ cup brown sugar

½ cup sea salt salt

2-3 tbsp honey

2 tbsp argan oil

2 tbsp fresh orange juice

Directions:

Mix all ingredients until you have a smooth paste. Apply to wet skin and exfoliate body in small, circular motions. Rinse with warm water.

Lavender Body Scrub Recipe

Ingredients:

1/2 cup sugar

2 tbsp lavender leaves

¼ cup jojoba oil

3 drops lavender essential oil

Directions:

Combine sugar and lavender leaves. Add jojoba oil and lavender essential oil. Apply the mixture to damp skin. Gently exfoliate in small, circular motions. Rinse with warm water.

Rosemary Body Scrub

Ingredients:

1/2 cup coconut oil

1/2 cup sugar

1/4 cup flax seeds

7-8 drops Rosemary Essential Oil

Directions:

Combine sugar and flax seeds and stir until mixed well. Add the coconut oil and mix until evenly combined. Apply the mixture to damp skin. Gently exfoliate in small, circular motions. Rinse with warm water.

Banana-Sugar Body Scrub

Ingredients:

1 ripe banana

4 tbsp raw sugar

1 tbsp cocoa powder

2 tbsp almond oil

¼ tsp pure vanilla extract

Directions:

Smash ingredients together with a fork. Gently massage over your body for a few minutes. Rinse off with warm water

Coffee Body Scrub

Ingredients:

1/4 cup ground coffee

1/4 cup sugar

3 tbsp olive oil

1 vitamin E capsule

Directions:

Mix sugar with ground coffee, olive oil and the Vitamin E capsule. Apply over wet body and massage gently. Rinse off with warm water.

Strained Yogurt Face Mask

Ingredients:

5 tbsp plain yogurt

1 slice of white bread

Directions:

This is a very old family recipe and is also the easiest basic face mask. It was used probably by every Bulgarian mother and grandmother back in the days when there were no commercial creams and moisturizers.

Place the slice of bread in a plate, put the yogurt on top of it, spread it evenly and leave in the fridge for a few hours or overnight. In the morning take the strained yogurt and spread it on your clean face, leave it for 20 minutes and rinse it with water. Results are always excellent.

Oats Bran Face Mask

Ingredients:

3 tbsp oats bran

hot water

2 drops Bulgarian rose essential oil

Directions:

Boil bran in 1/2 cup of water. Strain, cool, add rose oil and apply to face. Leave for 15 minutes and wash with lukewarm water.

Pear and Honey Mask

Ingredients:

1 ripe pear

1 tbsp honey

1 tsp sour cream

Directions:

Peel and cut the pear, then mash it with a fork into a smooth paste. Stir in a tablespoon of honey and a teaspoon of cream.

Spread the mixture evenly over your face and neck. Leave it for 10 minutes then rinse off.

Banana Nourishing Mask

Ingredients:

1 banana

1 tsp honey

1 tsp plain yogurt

Directions:

Mash a banana, add the honey and the yogurt, mix well and spread it evenly on a clean face. Leave it for at least 15 minutes and wash with cold water.

Apple Autumn Mask

Ingredients:

1/2 apple

1 tsp oatmeal

1 tsp honey

Directions:

Take a ripe half apple, grate it and mash it with a fork. Add one teaspoon oatmeal and one teaspoon honey to it and stir well.

Spread on face and leave it on until the mixture dries completely then rinse it off with ordinary water.

About the Author

Vesela lives in Bulgaria with her family of six (including the Jack Russell Terrier). Her passion is going green in everyday life and she loves to prepare homemade cosmetic and beauty products for all her family and friends.

Vesela has been publishing her cookbooks for over a year now. If you want to see other healthy family recipes that she has published, together with some natural beauty books, you can check out her Author Page on Amazon.

Made in the USA
Middletown, DE
29 April 2019